HOW THEY LIVED

A VICTORIAN FACTORY WORKER

STEWART ROSS

Illustrated by
Alan Langford

HOW THEY LIVED

A Family in World War II
A Medieval Serf
A Roman Centurion
A Victorian Factory Worker

First published in 1985 by
Wayland (Publishers) Limited
49 Lansdowne Place, Hove,
East Sussex, BN3 1HF, England

ISBN 0 85078 501 4

Typeset by Planagraphic Typesetters Limited
Printed in Italy by G. Canale & C.S.p.A., Turin
Bound in the UK by The Pitman Press

CONTENTS

THE END OF THE DAY

A thin woman walked slowly out of the iron factory gates. Two ragged children walked by her side. She held fast to their hands, for they seemed almost too tired to walk. The smaller child stumbled on the wet, cobbled streets.

It was already 9 o'clock at night. The woman paused outside a stall and bought a small loaf of bread for supper. The family had started work at seven that morning, and they had worked all day.

The woman and her children were factory workers in Victorian Britain. Victoria was Queen of Britain between 1837 and 1901, and during this time the country changed a great deal. The population grew from 19 million to 37 million. Britain became an industrial country, with most people living in towns, and working in factories or offices. When important things change very quickly we call it a revolution. An industrial revolution had taken place in Britain.

Steam engines took over from horses, water and wind as sources of power. They were fired by coal, and could drive much bigger machines. New coal mines were dug. Railways were built to carry coal and other goods. More and more factories sprang up, and there seemed to be more of everything each year in Victorian Britain.

A nineteenth-century iron foundry.

INDUSTRIAL CITIES

Victorian towns and cities grew very rapidly. In 1801 there were only four houses in Middlesbrough. By 1901 91,302 people lived there. Other towns grew fast, but London was by far the largest. By the end of Queen Victoria's reign its population was 4½ million.

The streets of Victorian cities were often thick with smog.

Houses for the workers were usually built close to the factories.

A modern town has very complicated services, such as sewers, street lights, a water supply, and rubbish collection. We take these things for granted. But in Victoria's time towns were not so well organized. Houses were built wherever there was space. The nearer one got to the centre of a city, the more squashed together the buildings were. Factories were built right next to houses and cottages. Often buildings were put up before anyone thought about a water supply or drains.

Early Victorian cities were like ants' nests. Everywhere men, women and children bustled about their business down narrow streets, or beside dirty rivers. The canal in Bradford was know as 'River Stink'.

Railway engines, factory steam engines, and fires in homes all used coal. This made thick black smoke. In the winter the smoke mixed with fog to make smog. Smog went everywhere, even into people's houses. The famous writer, Charles Dickens, said that living in London was like living in the clouds!

WORKERS' HOUSES

In most Victorian towns there were never enough houses. Factory workers sometimes had only one room for all the family. Very poor people had no houses at all. They lived in cellars, under bridges, or even in sewers.

Cottages were built for the workers near new factories. These small houses were often in long rows. One house was built on to the back of another, as you can see in the picture

Workers' houses were built back-to-back with no room for gardens.

on page 8. There were no gardens for the children to play in.

In some cities the houses for the workers were built round courtyards. The entrances to the yards were narrow tunnels. The houses were dark and damp and the courtyards were dirty. In 1833 Boot and Shoe Yard in Leeds was cleared out – seventy-five cartloads of filth were taken from this one little alley!

A slum in the industrial city of Glasgow in 1868.

Houses for the factory workers were usually built as quickly and as cheaply as possible. The walls were thin, and there were no foundations. Sometimes the floors were so weak that people fell through them into the room below! New houses soon turned into slums. Inside they became so wet that fungus grew on the ceilings and walls. In some towns there was only one water pump and one lavatory for a whole street.

Not all factory workers lived in slums, though. A few employers built comfortable houses for their workers. George Cadbury built a whole new village, called Bournville, for the people who were lucky enough to work in his chocolate factory.

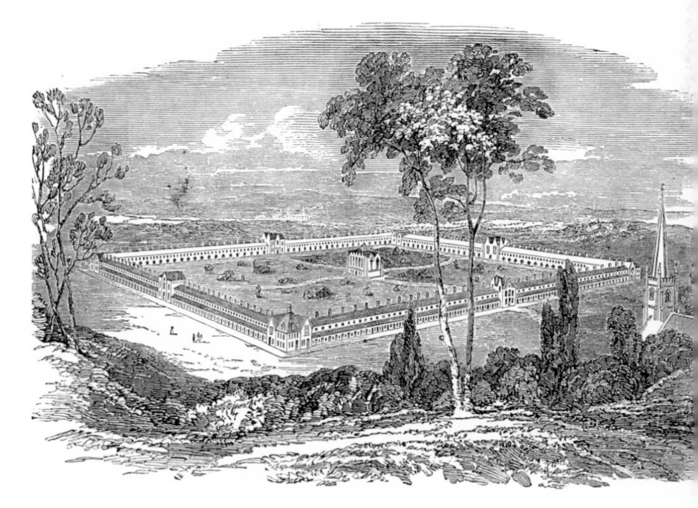

A sketch of a model village made in 1850. It was never built.

FAMILY LIFE

Factory workers usually had large families. A family of eight or nine children was not unusual. Children were born at home. In crowded, unhealthy houses many babies and children died of disease. Large funerals were popular in Victorian times. Everyone wore black, and boys with sad faces were hired to walk beside the coffin.

Workers often had to wait a long time to get married. It took them years to save enough money to set up home. Even then they could not afford to buy very much.

The whole town came to watch a funeral in Victorian times.

The father was the head of the Victorian family. Everyone else had to do what he said, especially the children. Fathers were often rather strict. Wives didn't go out to work if their husbands earned enough. Most men working in factories were not well paid, so their wives had to take jobs. Early in Victoria's reign children worked in factories too, often in awful conditions and for very long hours. This didn't leave much time for family life.

A typical Victorian worker's home was poorly furnished with just bare boards on the floor. Often there was just one room for the whole family.

The Factories

In the early nineteenth century factories were quite a new idea. Before then most things were made by hand in small workshops, or at home. However, during the industrial revolution there were several new inventions. Big machines for making cloth or iron goods did the work of many people. Steam engines and water wheels drove these machines.

Most of the men who owned the factories wanted to make as much money as possible. They paid the factory workers very little. A man might earn up to £1 a week. Some received only 10 shillings (50p).

Women and children were paid much less. Early in Victoria's reign women received as little as 5 shillings (25p) a week. Children were paid just one or two shillings.

As well as being paid very low wages, Victorian factory workers had to work very long hours. Children sometimes worked for fourteen or fifteen hours a day. They worked all day on Saturday, and sometimes on Sundays. Men had to slap and kick the children to keep them awake.

The inside of a factory was often too hot or too cold. The lighting was bad and there was little fresh air. The poor factory workers were just like pieces of machinery. In one factory they were even fined for talking to each other.

Left *Children being hired by factory owners in London in 1850.*

Right *Workers were paid as little as 10 shillings (50p) a week.*

LIFE AT WORK

Factory workers were carefully organized at work. Men called overlookers kept watch on everything that went on. The workers had to pay for broken machinery, and there were fines for poor work. Some employers changed the clocks to make people work longer.

Overlookers made sure that the factory workers arrived on time. A worker could be sacked for being late.

The biggest factories were in the textile industry. They made cotton and woollen goods. Here the men did the heavy work, carrying and loading. Women looked after the machines. They checked the quality, and made sure that there was enough thread. Children went around oiling the moving parts, or running errands.

It is wrong to think that all factory owners were cruel and greedy. Sir Titus Salt built good houses for the people who worked in his factory. He also gave them a school, a chapel, a park and built baths. But he would not let them drink alcohol. A few employers provided pensions, and pay for workers who were sick. Others gave them plenty of good food.

These workers are making matches at a factory in London.

Robert Owen was a factory owner who built good houses for his workers. This is his New Lanark factory.

Parliament also slowly helped the factory workers. In 1833 factory inspectors began to be used. They had to see that laws about children's work were being obeyed. A new law in 1844 said that guards had to be put around dangerous machinery. Another law in 1897 gave workers money if they were injured at work. But when Queen Victoria died in 1901 the life of a factory worker was still very hard. Not until 1911 did they all receive old age pensions from the state.

WORKERS' PROTEST

Some factory owners refused to make life more pleasant for people who worked for them. So groups of workers tried to help themselves. They joined societies, called trade unions. Members of a union promised to help each other.

Trade unions were allowed by the government in 1824. But the first big union, led by Robert Owen, was not very successful. Some workers grew angry that nothing was being done to help them. They tried to force Parliament to make changes. They said that working people should be in the government.

Parliament was given a huge petition, called the People's Charter. The thousands of people who signed it were called Chartists. But the government would not listen. By the end of 1848 the Chartists gave up.

So workers tried trade unions again. The best way to make an

Chartists carrying their petition to the House of Commons. It was signed by 3,317,702 people.

employer help them was for everyone to refuse to work. This is called a strike. Strikes were made legal by new laws passed in 1871 and 1875. The first very big strike was in 1889.

At the very end of Queen Victoria's reign workers formed their own political party. It was called the Labour Party. Keir Hardie was their first Member of Parliament. He had worked in a coal mine, so he was able to tell the government how hard life was for working people.

Workers are urged to join a trade union. Many were afraid to do so for fear of losing their jobs.

Food And Cooking

In the homes of the factory workers cooking was done on big stoves or open fires that burned coal or coke.

Above *Food was cooked on a stove or above an open fire.*

Some families baked their own bread in the oven. The pots and pans were heavy and made of black iron.

When a house did not have its own tap, all water had to be brought from outside in buckets. The houses did not have refrigerators or food mixers and there were no washing machines. Only large houses had kitchens.

There was no frozen or tinned food. Breakfast cereals, sliced bread and coffee powder had not been invented. The factory workers ate simple, dull meals, that were not always very good for them.

Below *Meals for workers were usually very simple and dull.*

project (4)

Here is an example of what a real Victorian family ate. Mr and Mrs Simpson, who lived in York, earned £5 a month. They spent half their money on food. These are the the family's meals for Wednesday, 21st February 1901:

Breakfast:	Dripping, toast and tea
Dinner:	Soup
Tea:	Meat, bread and tea

There were no vegetables, and no food for supper. Mr and Mrs Simpson and their three children must have gone to bed hungry that night.

The Victorians drank a great deal of gin and beer. This was the only luxury that poor people could afford. Many families spent more on drink than on their rent.

Many workers spent their spare time and money in gin palaces.

WORKERS' CLOTHES

Working women always tied their hair up to avoid catching it in the machines.

The picture on page 20 shows women working in a Victorian factory. You can see the long dresses that they wore then. Most of them have pinafores over their dresses to keep them clean. Ladies were not supposed to show more than their ankles. Some families even covered up piano legs, because they thought that they were rude. Factory workers could not afford many dresses. The very poor had just one, and it was often patched and darned.

Long dresses were difficult to work in. Sometimes they got caught in the factory machinery, and terrible accidents happened. Women also wore their hair long, so they had to tie this up for work. They wore strong boots and thick stockings. In the north of England some people still wore wooden clogs. Poor children sometimes had no shoes at all.

The clothes of men who worked in factories were like those of today. They wore trousers, shirts and jackets, but not pullovers. The only difference was that in Victorian times men always wore hats. Even the men working in the steel furnace in the picture on this page have their hats on — they must have been very hot.

Men usually wore a hat to work, even in a hot steel furnace like this one.

WORKERS' HEALTH

In 1899 Britain was fighting a war in South Africa. Half the men who wanted to join the army had to be turned away because they were not healthy enough.

The average age of death for a Victorian factory worker was about 30. Their houses, as we have seen, were unhealthy. The food they ate did not build them up properly. They did not have enough money to pay for a doctor's visit. There were very few hospitals, and most of them were places where people went to die. Horrible diseases thrived in the dirty cities. In the narrow streets they spread quickly. Cholera killed many thousands of people in three terrible outbreaks in 1831-33, 1847-8 and 1865-6.

Hospitals were often unhygenic places where people went to die. Wards were huge with few doctors.

Project 4

The factory workers were in danger at work too. Look at all the dangerous machinery in the factory in the picture on this page.

Slowly life did get better during the nineteenth century. Parliament made laws which allowed local councils to clean up the towns and cities. Other laws stopped children working in factories. Some important discoveries were made which improved people's health. Antiseptics were introduced in 1865. Chloroform, which enabled doctors to put people to sleep during an operation, was first used in 1847. Before they had had to lie and watch the surgeon at work.

Many factory workers were killed or injured by dangerous machinery.

Religion and Recreation

Wealthy Victorians were very religious. Families went to church or chapel every Sunday, and they held family prayers each day. The factory workers were not like this at all.

In 1851 all the people who went to a Sunday service were counted. The result was a great shock. Most working people either stayed at home, or were at work. There were not enough churches for them in the new cities. They felt that religion was only for the rich.

The most popular recreation for factory workers was drinking. Until the 1870s pubs were open all day, and anyone could buy a drink. In late Victorian times football became very popular. Many of today's clubs started then. The players wore strange long trousers. Workers also went to cricket matches, and on bank holidays they visited parks and heaths.

By the 1890s better-paid factory workers were able to afford train tickets to the seaside. They had longer holidays as well. But they still wore their hot, heavy clothes on the beach, as you can see in the picture.

Left *A Victorian family at the seaside.*

Right *Victorian churches were mostly filled with rich people.*

CRIME AND PUNISHMENT

Crime was a serious problem in Victorian times. There was not enough work for everyone, and there was no unemployment pay. So poor people had to steal money to buy food. Factory workers were tempted to steal because they were not paid enough.

In 1867 about 100,000 criminals lived in London. There were pickpockets, horse-stealers, forgers and muggers. They made life difficult for honest workers. The police were not very efficient either. In the middle of Victoria's reign several cities had no full time policemen.

Poor people often had to turn to crime to earn enough money to eat.

These are female convicts at Brixton prison in 1862.

Project 7

For serious crimes, such as murder, a criminal was hung. Another common punishment was transportation. This meant sending a guilty person to Australia. This country had only just been discovered, and life there was very tough.

The Victorians built many new prisons. They were all very grim places. In one the prisoners were so hungry that they ate worms. In another prisoners were beaten if they looked at each other.

One girl ran away from her factory because it was so horrible. She was caught, and sent to prison for seven months as a punishment.

People who went to prison for debt had the most difficult time. They were not freed until they had paid their debts. But in prison they could not earn any money. So they often stayed in jail until they died.

Victorian prisons were built to be as grim as possible to stop people committing crimes.

A Time Of Change

Life for factory workers changed a great deal during Victoria's long reign. We have seen how discoveries helped to improve health. The invention of electric light made factories brighter and safer. Parliament stopped young children being employed. Adults were not allowed to work for too long each day; machinery was fenced off; workers joined unions to protect themselves.

Some of the big towns had been cleaned up. Joseph Chamberlain was mayor of Birmingham between 1873 and 1876. During this time slums

Towards the end of the Victorian period people had more leisure time.

were pulled down, and new sewers were built. Street lights were set up, and many homes were given clean running water.

By the time Queen Victoria died factory workers enjoyed summer holidays. More men in Parliament were trying to help them. Important laws of 1884 and 1885 gave many working people the vote. This meant that they could help choose who went to Parliament.

Families were smaller at the end of the nineteenth century. Careful workers were able to save a little money. Some bought bicycles, and travelled on them into the countryside. They might have met one of the new motor cars that had just been invented.

By 1900 factory workers were no longer just machines. The cruelty and squalor of early Victorian Britain had gone for ever.

Workers could sometimes save enough money to buy a bicycle.

THE WORKSHOP OF THE WORLD

In the nineteenth century Britain was the most powerful country in the world. The British navy ruled the waves. Other countries were conquered and forced to join the British Empire. This happened because Britain became industrialized before any other country. This made her very rich. Her manufactured goods were sold to many countries, and she was called 'the workshop of the world'.

The Victorian factory workers made this wealth, but they did not share it. Their lives were short, sad and poor. Britain today is not as powerful as it was in Victoria's time. But for most people it is a much better place to live in.

Britain was once called 'The Workshop of the World', but most of her workers were very poor.

Glossary

Antiseptic A medicine that kills germs.
Clog A wooden-soled shoe.
Council The people who run a town or city.
Forge To make false money.
Foundations The base of a building.
Government The people who run a country.
Parliament The place where people meet to talk about how the country should be run.
Pension Money paid to someone after they have retired.
Pinafore A long apron.
Population The number of people living somewhere.
Slum A dirty and run-down house or street.
Squalor Dirty and unpleasant conditions.

More Books to Read

Penelope Davies, *Children of the Industrial Revolution* (Wayland 1972)
Molly Harrison, *Growing up in Victorian Days* (Wayland, 1980)
Frank E. Huggett, *A Day in the Life of a Victorian Factory Worker* (Allen and Unwin, 1973)
W. J. Reader, *Life in Victorian England* (Batsford)
Alastair Scott, *One Day In Victorian England* (Tyndall, 1974)

INDEX

Picture acknowledgements

The pictures in this book were supplied by the following: E. T. Archive 30; The Mansell Collection 7, 9 (left), 10, 12, 13 (top and bottom), 18 (left), 28; Mary Evans Picture Library 5, 18 (right), 21, 23, 24. The remaining pictures are from the Wayland Picture Library. Hand tinting by Nick Cannon.